AN ANTHOLOGY OF RAIN

BOOKS BY PHILLIS LEVIN

POETRY

Temples and Fields

The Afterimage

Mercury

May Day

Mr. Memory & Other Poems

An Anthology of Rain

AS EDITOR

*The Penguin Book of the Sonnet:
500 Years of a Classic Tradition in English*

AN ANTHOLOGY OF RAIN

POEMS

Phillis Levin

BARROW STREET PRESS
NEW YORK CITY

©2025 by Phillis Marna Levin
All rights reserved

Cover Art: Julian Hatton
Cover Design: Joel W. Coggins
Interior Design: Michelle Caraccia

Published 2025 by Barrow Street, Inc., New York City
(501) (c) (3) corporation. All contributions are tax deductible.
Distributed by:
Barrow Street Books
c/o University of Rhode Island
English Department, Swan 114
60 Upper College Road
Kingston, RI 02881

Barrow Street Books are also distributed by Itasca Books Distribution & Fulfillment, 210 Edge Place, Minneapolis MN, 55418, itascabooks.com. Telephone (844) 488-4477; amazon.com; Ingram Periodicals Inc., 1240 Heil Quaker Blvd, PO Box 7000, La Vergne, TN 37086-700 (615) 213-3574; and Armadillo & Co., 7310 S. La Cienega Blvd, Inglewood, CA 90302, (310) 693-6061.

Special thanks to the University of Rhode Island English Department and especially the PhD Program in English, 60 Upper College Road, Swan 114, Kingston, RI 02881, (401) 874-5931, which provides valuable in-kind support, including graduate and undergraduate interns.

First Edition

Library of Congress Control Number 2024950155 (print)

ISBN 9781962131063 (paperback)   ISBN 9781962131087 (ebook)

For Jack

and in memory of my parents,
Herbert Louis Levin & Charlotte Shirley Engel Levin

CONTENTS

AN ANTHOLOGY OF RAIN	3
BLUEPRINT	5
CONTENTMENT	8
EVENING WALK	9
MORONI'S TAILOR	11
TO A NEW CHAIR	15
BOUNTY	16
WOMAN WASHING A STREET IN DELFT	17
KETTLE	20
MAN IN RED SHOES	21
MAPMAKERS: A SKETCH	23
DUEL OF ROSES	24
UNDEVELOPED NEGATIVES	28
METAMORPHOSIS	30
EAR OF CORN	32
SEPTEMBER FIRST AGAIN	33
CHAMBER	34
LIGHT METER	35
HE RETURNS	36
IN A VALLEY	37
NARCISSUS	38

SECRET RITES	39
HOW IT IS	42
HAT SAGA	44
WALLPAPER POEM	47
A TREE IN EARLY MARCH	49
BURBLE	50
ANCIENT STORY	51
THEOREMS OF REASON	53
GIACOMETTI'S SHADOW	54
A GROWL	55
RIDDLE	57
BULL'S-EYE	58
FOR METKA	60
OCTOBER STORM	61
DECEMBER TANKA	62
ORB	63
WOODEN SPOON	64
Notes	69
Acknowledgments	73
About the Author	77

There is another world, and it is in this one.

—Paul Éluard

Depth must be hidden. Where? On the surface.

—Hugo von Hofmannsthal

AN ANTHOLOGY OF RAIN

AN ANTHOLOGY OF RAIN

For this you may see no need,
You may think my aim
Dead set on something

Devoid of conceivable value:
An Anthology of Rain,
A collection of voices

Telling someone somewhere
What it means to follow a drop
Traveling to its final place of rest.

But do consider this request
If you have pressed your nose
Of any shape against a window,

Odor of metal faint, persistent,
While a storm cast its cloak
Over the shoulder of every cloud

In sight. You are free to say
Whatever crosses your mind
When you look at the face of time

In the passing of one drop
Gathering speed, one drop
Chasing another, racing to

A fork in the path, lingering
Before making a detour to join
Another, fattening on the way

Until entering a rivulet
Running to the sill.
So please accept this invitation:

You are welcome to submit,
There is no limit to its limit,
The instructions are a breeze

As long as you include
Nothing about yourself,
Even your name. Your address

Remains unnecessary, for the rain
Will find you—if you receive it
It receives you (whether or not

You contribute, a volume
Is sent). And when you lift
The collection you may hear,

By opening anywhere, a drop
And its story reappear
As air turns to water, water to air.

BLUEPRINT

The poem I want to build needs a vestibule
Inviting all who wish to be bidden
Welcome: an ample parallelogram
With a skylight open to a patch of stars.

Horses, of course there will be horses
Gathering in darkness
Under those stars in a field of grass
Extending far enough for an eye to grasp

Bounty uncontainable. A passageway
Will lead to a loft for the hay
And a wing to accommodate the rain.
Where will I store a roomful of ash?

In a crypt in the cellar,
Adjoining vaulted chambers of seed
Saved from flowers buried
In pockets in a dream. The attic

Is for scores of unheard music,
Notes from expired currencies, toys,
Diplomas, film reels, a shoebox of shells,
Centuries of things to be sorted later

(Albums, letters, keys, locks of hair),
Sealed to keep the past from taking over.
Essential to the structure is an atrium
Where a thought on its own may rise,

And every storey shall include
Corners tempting a child to hide.
What the garden grows, a resident,
However transient, may decide,

Provided some hydrangeas recollect
Slow-dissolving cumuli
And along a gate unlatched for passersby
Lobelias spill indigo.

Above all, the plan will correspond
With the terrain beyond the boundary,
Features of topography the print alone
Won't show (a void

Is a wilderness sustained
By the margin). To that end,
The design makes sure a visitor
Exiting any door must meander,

Following light as it falls across
Nameless shades in a palette of moss
On a path sown with conifer needles until
Stumbling into a clearing

Before a precipice, whose lip
Offers access to
Water on water pouring through
A stone vestibule—
                Here, I'm at a loss,

Without a line to plumb the measure of bliss.
But I know this: when I step outside
There's a space within reach
No quadrant can divine or divide.

CONTENTMENT

Exhales a note, a bullfrog
Bellows, a mallard finds its mate

On another shore. And in the rushes,
No rushing, unless the rustle
Of wing on water counts.

So a day is spent, unspent, spinning
A web from bough to bough,

Ample enough to entertain a rainbow,
Nimble enough to balance a bead
Of dew, another momentary globe.

EVENING WALK

Stutter of sparks
From fireworks
Somewhere in the distance

Too distant to hear

Flecks swarming
Through branches
Scattering

Here and there
A stray streamer

It's only the lightning bugs
Rising from the meadow

Settled now
In the marsh grass

Blinking

And a skull aglow
Down the road
On a crumbled wall

Is nothing more
Than what remains
Of a wild turkey egg

Abandoned by a scavenger
Not long ago

Looking chastens us

West Cornwall, Connecticut

MORONI'S TAILOR

Il Tagliapanni (c. 1570)
—GIOVANNI BATTISTA MORONI

On a black cloth, a line of chalk
Marks the course my scissors must follow.

    You follow its path, dabbing
    At your palette, tending to my likeness

Faithfully, until stepping back into the light
Taking you further each day

    From the weight of your father's toolbox:
    Chisels and mallet set in separate chambers,

Plans translated by sweat into columns, arches,
Turrets, tombs. Your unerring hand

    Proves you are his son, though you combine
    Powder and oil instead of sand and lime—

And you abide by a tempo that dwells
Not in the ring of steel on marble, but a bell

    Calling the quarter hour, thickening the air
    The people of Albino move within

Before dispersing, going home to evening prayer,
Yielding to pigeons that occupy the square,

    Waves of them changing patterns at every
    Turn, as if design, not direction,

Were all that matters. You prefer to face
Each face alone: a gentleman in pink brocade

    Standing with a sword by a ruined wall,
    A lady in solemn jet

Whose finger keeps her place in a book of verse
Written by another noble sitter (in the grey

    Lining of her sleeve, the layer
    Of lace at his wrist, my skill

As well as yours resides). You would rather
Alter an angle to sharpen character,

    Render a gaze defying decay, disarming
    Any of us who enter where they

Live on, carrying their immaculate dignity
Into our uncertain future. Bergamo is falling

    To strangers, the Republic divided,
    Even the churches are not free of blood.

You lean your canvas on an easel,
I stretch my fabric on a table. You dress them

> In the Spanish fashion, cutting darkness
> From darkness. So do I.

Here is material fit for a man
Who stays away from the clash of knives,

> Avoids an oath that could end in war
> Or the stain of exile. Today, Giovanni,

I prepare the cloth: you have given
My semblance a soul, done justice to my form,

> Shown the bare room where I reign—
> But see to the ruffle at my throat

So they know how far I have come. (Better
To remain in Albino, beyond the noise of fame.)

> Aloof as a courtesan, Venice once
> Displayed herself to me in an alley

Where I met a merchant selling the finest silk:
Visible from the door of his little shop,

> An immense flag billowed on a façade
> Across the canal, a stone's throw

From where I stood. I paused at the same spot
Later, savoring my acquisition, a weave

      Embroidered with silver thread.
      But the banner beckoned—liquid

In the wind, then familiar. It was the crest
Of your favorite patron, whose doublet

      Needed new buttons for Carnival
      (I saved a piece of velvet for them).

When I couldn't reach the palace on foot
Or find a gondolier to row me there,

      That rippling emblem, mutable
      As flame, mutable as water,

Seemed like a garment meant for a time
Hereafter. Obscurity may be no more

      Than a phantom obstruction, my friend,
      An error of sight, just as a shadow

May cast the shape of a chasm,
Portending depth though nothing is below.

      Today my scissors follow the chalk,
      Tomorrow I will help you make your name.

TO A NEW CHAIR

The room is ready for you, dear.
I've cleared everything out,
Whatever is left is yours.

From now on, I'm beside the point.
As long as I sit still,
Your wings will carry me far.

BOUNTY

What I have found is
Nothing suffices as much
As a single crumb.

WOMAN WASHING A STREET IN DELFT

How long have you been
On your knees? You seem by now
To belong in that position,
Obeying the law of your maker,

Whose sheen of attention renders
Every burden dear. You attend
To the stones: some of them glint,
Some refuse to surrender their grit

No matter how hard you scrub,
All gain luster equally—given
A good washing. There's a package
On the doorstep, where you kneel

Without looking up. Whose door
Is it? What more is there to see?
Low land, low sky, a spire
Jutting into clouds that dwindle

Into curds. A bucket of water
Beside you grows colder, heavier
Than that child born early
Today, so you heard,

When across the canal a voice
Calling out spread the word.
For now you remain unknown,
Facing away from view

On a street familiar as rain:
Your shape a cipher, your bonnet
A new moon in winter, whatever
Lingers in you (weight of water,

Click-click of pattens on shoes,
Waves of scent from linen drying,
From a load of herring on the quay)
Possible to fathom

Only by skimming the surface
Where you appear. Off the record
You survive, not ruined or stolen,
Among the missing, hidden,

Forgotten: concealed by a curtain
Finer than any shawl that touches
Your skin. So long you have been
Kept in a windowless hall

In a villa on a foreign square,
Maiden of loss waiting to be shown
To the world. I saw you once, under-
Stood in a breath (after the veil

Was lifted) that you are no one
In particular, priceless
As sight, a share in the ongoing
Trade-off of money for light,

Your value rising each day
Until the sun burns out. You need
Or seem to need to scour clean
Your allotted portion

Of a scene—or did I misread you
Completely? Could you be a girl
In the dress of a woman, caught
By her father, Johannes Vermeer,

Unlatching a window
To find one of his children at play?
Whoever you are, kneeling figure,
Daughter, sister, mother, little

Patch of color, dwelling
On the cobblestones, toiling
Away, you continue to be
Unaccounted for.

KETTLE

Flame under the bubbling water.
Blue flame. Water ready for tea.

Amber infusion soon to be seeping,

Leaves about to uncurl. Here
Is a tin, a spoon, a cup, an open

Teapot saying, *Nobody else but me*
To nobody else but you: awaken,

Pour. What are you waiting for?

MAN IN RED SHOES

There's a man in red shoes across the street
Right now. Moments ago a bird
Hopped from one leaf to another, flew
Zigzag to a different branch still

Within sight. The man in red shoes is there
No longer: all I did was look away
To record what I saw, and he was gone.
No record other than this

Of that moment, of the stray white fluff
Drifting on a current barely lifting
A cluster of late summer leaves
Belying the illusion that the air was still.

It wasn't still. And he's gone, not resting
Anymore against the low stone wall
Dividing the road from the park.
When he looked at my window

A few storeys up, I didn't call out
Or give a sign of acknowledgment,
Although it seemed our eyes had met
Before he turned away. The bird

That visited the bough, the floating
Tuft of a seed, and he who stood
Inside those shoes, left
Without leaving a mark,

Transporting themselves
Where they needed to be.

MAPMAKERS: A SKETCH

If you look at them, they appear to be meaningless squiggles and scrawls or practice sheets for someone learning cursive. In fact, they are maps and mazes. The only way out. Drawings understood to be going nowhere—all the same, essential for survival.

That was the beginning, a begging for a door, a route outside.

There was an *outside* outside the window; there wasn't any access to it, except for those squiggles and scrawls, lines in a notebook whose black & white marbled cover belied a forest within, rampant with birdsong and moss and the burble of a brook we would follow to its source once we were there.

Together we sat on the floor, brother and sister filling the time. Filling cold-to-the-touch faintly ruled pages, poring over them, turning a leaf to begin another foray into the world. Starting again. Taking turns. If you looked at us, we would appear to be going nowhere, taking turns doing nothing of consequence, making a meaningless script.

Look at them, children in a maze making mazes ending nowhere. Illegible as the future. Notebooks filled with time. Carbon from their pencils adding the slightest change in weight. It's time to open them, turn those unreadable leaves.

DUEL OF ROSES

Once in the streets of Rome
I engaged in a duel of roses,
en garde, en garde,

with Veronica Piraccini,
painter of the invisible,
connoisseur of a way to conjure
color in darkness,

who would hold her mamma's
antique Parmesan grater
between her knees,

a madonna in a fury
working that contraption
to amass a cloud of cheese

as she made a midnight
carbonara for herself and me.

She talked a mile a minute
(a kilometer, should I say),
peppering her Italian
with *over-the-top,*

the only expression in English
she ever used, a subtitle
for the comedy of her life,

while I, drunk on an excess
of vowels, held my tongue
lest she scrape her skin
or fail to check the boiling water

if a bout of mutual laughter
were to begin.

What was the spur of this humor?
Nothing less than the trouble
her beauty got her in,

one adventure after another
ending in a *disastro*—
flourishes of gallantry
followed by bad behavior.

How did we get those flowers?
We found a fresh bouquet
someone must have flung,
who knows why,

over the rail of a café
we'd soon be strolling by.

Rose in hand I raised my arm
to the sky, *en garde,*
en garde, and she,
rose in hand, raised hers.

From the outside,
how did our duel appear?

We didn't care:
we upheld our honor,
defending our right to be there
no matter the hour.

Late it was
when we parried on the bridge

where a pope sought refuge
crossing, where the stems
of our roses crossed.

I can still hear the horns blow
in the shadow of Sant'Angelo
(Bernini's angels in a row,
one holding Veronica's veil)—

and a boy calling out to Veronica,
Che bella, che bella,
Marilyn Monroe,
from a wingèd scooter on the go

in the year of the Great Jubilee
at the close of the last century,
2000 *anno Domini,*

zeros lining up anew,
a trail of pilgrims murmuring,
jostling, streaming through.

UNDEVELOPED NEGATIVES

In a box on a shelf out of reach
They sleep, far from the spices and dust of Cairo,
Where a girl of fifteen, soon to marry,
Interrupted all who gathered, blurting
Across the dinner table a statement that meant
What she didn't mean: *I love you,* she said,

Looking at me as every mouth moving
Stopped, her English cutting through coils
Of German braided with Arabic and French,
Her sentence a small glinting knife.
Then, gentle laughter, platters syllables spoons
On a wave of saffron, cumin, mint.

She took me aside the next day
To show her trousseau, opened a box
Filled with linen and lace, and a necklace
Nestled in silk, confessing this wasn't her first
Engagement. Her father, she said,
Her father the gardener (we could see him

From a window) had just remarried, her new
Stepmother was only a year older than her,
She wanted *to study,* she wanted—she climbed
On top of a chair, imploring me to take
Her picture, pleading, *Take me*
With you, take me with you, standing there.

All that I took of her
Is somewhere in a box on a shelf out of reach
In the New York dark: she stands on a chair,
How she wanted me to picture her,
Remember her, why that way I'll never know
—And where is she now, on her lips

What curse, what prayer? What promise
Never offered, never kept, keeps her
Company at night, adrift in the perfume
Of cardamom and rose water, while her hope
Resides on a roll of film, curled
In its canister, untouched by light.

METAMORPHOSIS

As if to recreate
The plenitude of that laughing table,
Hands, so many hands
Reaching toward a bowl of labneh
To dip a piece of pita into a swirl

Of oil sprinkled with za'atar;
As if to replicate to some degree
The savor of that afternoon,
Oasis of kindness welcoming me
After a walk in the desert,

They made a promise to blend
The same combination of herbs
And sesame, and send the packet
By sea, given the list of things
No one can bring into my country.

So began its long journey
From a port in Egypt to Manhattan's
Port of entry, arriving at my door
Eventually, wrapped in plain paper,
A promise almost forgotten now

Fulfilled—and unsealing the parcel
I beheld, in a plastic baggie,
A thousand thousand larvae
Teeming pulsing
Without a sound, as if obeying

A command to be fruitful
And multiply, replenish the earth
And outnumber the stars
In the sky and have dominion
Over every living thing and terrify.

EAR OF CORN

An ear of corn
In a gust of wind,
Stirred from slumber,

Rustles, beads of gold
Bubbling under
A tangle of silky hair.

So many others fill
The same field, row
By row, one by one,

Repeating a rumor
Started by the sun.
A stalk of corn

Guards the dawn,
Umber tassel
Glistening, blade

Uplifted, listening:
Thy will be done,
Thy will be done.

SEPTEMBER FIRST AGAIN

Blighted light at the tip
Of a branch, why so early
Do you turn?—leaf
Dipped in vermilion,
Close to the end, you point
To a sidewalk wet
Once with names
Signed in cement to seal,
For all time, a vow
Uttered by two
Standing under the crown
Of a tree you cleave to still,
For now: solitary witness
Standing alone, limbs
Crisscrossing in shadows
Beginning to scrawl
Lines to a world hell-
Bent (with or without intent)
On obscuring
Whatever they meant.
Blighted light
At the topmost bough,
Little flag hailing
Another day, do not go
So early to ruin, green,
Do not turn so soon.

CHAMBER

The heart at the heart of the room
Hasn't stopped. When it does,

The room will go on
Being a room, without heart.

The room has a life of its own
Apart from breath, a breath apart.

LIGHT METER

A father wants his daughter to pose:
She doesn't want to,
Doesn't want to be caught, though

One day she will wish she'd been
Willing to stand inside time

Just a moment for him,
As he one day will stand with her
Outside time, adjusting a lens.

HE RETURNS

Do you think I don't know what it's like to come back
After being down there, alone
Without her? You who were born
With a spark of my soul, your face calling forth

My boyhood visage, listen when I say
There's nothing you could have done,
Cast off your sorrow.
However much she tormented me, to the end

We were together. Now I am gone,
Telling you what you must hear:
It doesn't matter that each day was hell—
Better to be near her than live in peace.

You, born from a spark of my soul, remember this
Whoever accompanies you,
Whatever befalls, whether fire or water
Engulfs the ground you tread.

Do not grieve that I am not at rest.
How can I stay away when she keeps calling?

IN A VALLEY

Grief freely flowing,
Like water down a mountain
From a glacier feeding

A brook snowbound,
Like song unbroken.
Blood in a channel going

Back to a heart borne back
To the heart of a mountain,
Back to the bank, to the bed.

NARCISSUS

When I thought it bottomless,
This sorrow, I found nothing
But light pouring more
Light from the mouth of a cup
Spilling its own spring.

SECRET RITES

On my bedroom's oak floor, when I was three, lay two oval rugs spaced several feet apart, the same intertwining flowers and leaves woven into them, the same pale fringe surrounding their borders. Those rugs became two islands: I would sit on one and, without standing up, move to the other without touching the floor. From one island to the other, without falling into the water. In summer, when heat and humidity interrupted my sleep, I'd crawl out of bed and lie on the floor, resting my cheek on the blessedly cool wood surface, ignoring the rules about drowning.

*

When my parents took me shopping for clothes, I'd wander off sometimes. At some point I'd reach into a coat pocket or the seam of a garment to find a stray thread and take it out—careful not to snag the fabric, simply removing what no longer was necessary. Winter coats were especially good. I would hold the thread and, still concealed from view, place it in one of my own pockets or wrap it around a button on my blouse. Or I'd pull a stray thread from something I was wearing and place it in the pocket of a coat I admired; this way, I could be elsewhere, live inside that pocket wherever it would go. What thrilled the most was knowing someone might buy this coat, that the two of us would be joined, my thread carried by whoever wore that coat. Unrelated threads, connected. A remnant. Relic of the impossible. Would anyone reach into this pocket one day and discover a thread that didn't belong?

*

I am a child no longer, away from home at last. A friendship starts in an instant, an affinity grasped at first sight, a word not yet spoken: knowledge tangible as an electrical charge. Within a week we are talking every day; she reads my poems, sets some of them to music. One evening, as we sit across from each other in the campus pub, a candle between us on the table, the slowly burning flame suddenly goes out. I strike a match to reignite the candle, and we notice how the flame leaps from the matchhead to the wick, jumping an unexpected distance. That's when the experiment, which will become our daily ritual, begins: we take turns blowing out the candle, holding a lit match as far from the wick as possible to see how far the little flame can travel. Most marvelous of all is when the flame traces a circuitous path. A jolt of joy united us when the vapor trail was lit and a new flame leapt to the wick. In the future, on the rare occasion that I demonstrate this phenomenon to anyone, it is met with surprise.

The following spring, she decided to cut the thread between us, break the attachment, put out the candle. The sentence on our friendship was passed without warning or recourse. We lose touch. She is ahead of me by two years. Unexpectedly, she appears at my graduation ceremony: we embrace under a sheer blue sky, never see each other again. Later I hear she has enrolled in a seminary, has taken vows and is a nun. Recently, at the frayed end of a search trailing many tangled threads, I find a series of essays she has published, and from a biographical note learn she is an Orthodox Christian monastic and pastoral counselor, abbess of a monastery dedicated to fostering reconciliation. Missing thread; thread of flame. Should I call her, write to her—or let the severed thread dangle?

*

My students laugh in one of our Zoom poetry workshops, a bit of relief during the pandemic. We've let our guard down, tell silly stories about things we did in childhood: I've encouraged them to recall visual memories. I confess my ritual of the two oval rugs—the agility required to avoid any part of my body touching the floor, a death by drowning. "The floor is lava!" one of them calls out from a square somewhere on my screen. I don't understand what they're talking about, why they can't stop laughing, until a student explains that The Floor Is Lava is a game they played as children, its rules akin to the rules I had established—except that the floor is molten rock instead of water.

*

These days, I touch the floor and do not drown.

*

Have you ever put your hand in your pocket and found a thread that doesn't belong?

HOW IT IS

Say how it is
How easy
Too easy to say

How it is
Is not how it is
It keeps changing

Before it becomes
A *was* already it *is*
Something

Altogether else
Say nothing it may
Stay still

How to say nothing
And say how it is
A bubble on a lake

Breaks in the dark
A streetlight goes on
Somewhere else an

Elastic band snaps
It burns a moment
To say how it is (say

How it is) to touch
The quivering
Hand of chance.

HAT SAGA

Why did I choose to wear that hat?
It was bitter cold, that's why I wore
The glamorous fur: it covered enough
Of my head to render me anonymous
(I didn't mean to look mysterious).

After the party we hailed a cab, happily
Sped, warm together in the dark until,
On an unfamiliar block, the taxi
Stopped, not a sign or a red light in sight.
Why did you stop? my husband said,

As a man out of nowhere appeared,
Like a character in a sinister plot,
Approaching the door
On the side of the car where I sat—
His face swimming close to the glass

Between us, window he knocked on
With the knuckles of his hand, a window
That I, too startled to do anything
But look him in the eye,
Began to roll down, roll down,

When in an instant he could see
A face he caught sight of
In silhouette: he must have taken me
For someone else, what sort of person,
What kind of woman, I do not know.

The hat, the hat, because of the hat
He saw someone he wanted
Or didn't want to see, he was waiting
For her or never wanted to see her
Again, she had something he needed,

A message to relay, she owed him
Something, was there just then
For a rendezvous, or there
By chance, not expecting him
To find her, and the hat, *my* hat,

Was the dead giveaway
Of her identity. If I took off my hat
He would have known right away
Who I was not. All at once
He un-saw what he had seen,

My ignorance of who he was,
The danger of his innocent mistake,
Evident without a doubt (his jaw,
A flicker around his jaw palpable).
And he said *Go,*

Releasing us into the night,
Touching the car door
As if breaking a spell.
Why did you stop? said my husband,
Once more, as soon as the cab took off.

I thought he was an undercover cop
Asking me to pull over, replied the driver.
Through streets of neon ice and snow
We fled, until Jack and I were home,
Safe in bed, though I, sleepless

Beside my sleeping mate, couldn't stop
Wondering who he thought he saw
Before the window rolled open
—What did and didn't happen
Inside the moment between—

Couldn't, for the life of me,
His face in the glass unsee.

Wallpaper Poem

If to dust we return
And we do
Why spend a minute
Choosing wallpaper
Patterns exquisite or dull

Will be dust as well
You may say
It will say as well to you
When you ponder

Fruit upon branches
Delaying the end
Trellises and semblances
Meeting meant-to-be
Seams and angles

Repeating what it is worth
To forget another hour
Lose oneself in a labyrinth
Devoid of a minotaur

What door never opened
Opens once and for all
If only you find
A flaw hidden in the design
Disclosing a moment

Time's timeless print
Gone now Here tomorrow
Deer at the edge of a wood
Turning still

A TREE IN EARLY MARCH

Out again, no trace
Of irony, a grace note
Upon every twig.

BURBLE

a found poem

To *burble* is to move
with a rippling flow, the way water
bubbles down the side of a small garden
waterfall.
        A stream burbles as it travels
along its bed, bubbling over
rocks and branches. The verb *burble* captures
both the movement of the water and the sound
it makes as it moves.
                Purl is the murmuring
sound, or the act of murmuring; or the gold
or silver thread or wire for embroidering or
edging; or the intertwisting of thread
that knots a stitch, usually
along an edge.
        To *burble*
is to move with a rippling flow,
purl is the murmuring sound or the act
of murmuring (sometimes along an edge).

ANCIENT STORY

In the war between the vast and the small, the minuscule win, the scales tip, infinitesimals prevail. Though hope does not yet exist, nor despair, their victory seems empty, for they are too minute to be seen, let alone remembered. Some gather out of necessity (if necessity can be said to rule in such a realm) and assemble into sums that in time multiply into alliances big enough to leave a mark. To a human eye, these odd-angled entities resemble ruins in a landscape translated by decay: up close, colossal characters; from afar, a scattering of runes, an alphabet without a key. Is a message there to be decoded, or left unread? That is a question for the future.

For reasons unknown, many of the tiniest organisms fail to join a colony, partake of any union. They abide in isolation, invisible motorized forms not alive not dead, unable (one cannot say unwilling) to forsake themselves to create a larger creature. On little or nothing they survive, flourishing undetected: in time they enter, by chance or of necessity, the bodies of other beings. Some make peace, some havoc, the former restoring order or serving as go-betweens, the latter engaging in acts of piracy or mass destruction (their infamy endures in dates engraved on monuments and fading tombstones, and in tomes tracing recurrent reigns of terror). In their own way they are immortal, at least for now.

A great number of the abovementioned loners behave like gracious guests, giving freely more than they take, improving the general atmosphere wherever they happen to dwell; indeed, to expel the uninvited, even those arousing unrest, may cause substantial harm to a host. Due to certain flaws in classification, the venomous, the beneficent, and the benign are commonly confused. Thus in most cases it is impossible to foresee how things will turn out in their presence. But whatever the case, good and evil, guilt and innocence, shall remain for them a far cry away.

May 2019

THEOREMS OF REASON

Hello to the theorems of reason, hidden
For so many years. How good to see them
Ready already to make trouble,
Bounce against the wall of each belief, level
Their aim at anything they mean to conquer.
Do you think you'll escape their rancor,
Or have you been practicing so hard
Nothing they say can cancel your parade?

Steel yourself for the next charade,
Contortions, clichés, incoherent banter,
Ideas betrayed, failing to pay rent or
Sell themselves on an open market: bubble
After bubble iridescent over rubble
Only the gold of the moon may redeem.

GIACOMETTI'S SHADOW

Trembles on a wall,
Lengthens on a stair, crosses
A moor, free to dwell
Eternally anywhere
Clay can be lit by a star.

A GROWL

Corkscrew Swamp Sanctuary, southwest Florida

Not loud,
But deeper than a lion's roar
Under the very spot
On which we stood:

Never heard a noise like that before,
Never felt a fear like that before
Rumbling through us,
Uniting us even more.

We had strolled a while on the boardwalk,
Passing ancient cypresses
Scarred by fire or drought,
When the sound of a creaky hinge

Of a door opening closing
Drew our attention skyward
To a molting anhinga opening
Shutting, opening shutting its wings

On a limb overhanging the swamp.
That's what made us notice
A congregation of baby gators
Basking on a log in the shallows,

Oblivious to danger, no mother,
No father in sight.
                    The growl
Shook every cell of the planks
Below our feet, arising

From a source we couldn't identify
Until peering over the edge we saw,
Peeking out, its unmistakable
Eyes and snout.

We, who intended no harm,
Set off its alarm—
One step from being dragged
Into the water to our demise,

In which case the anhinga
Would be our living witness.

RIDDLE

This
Doesn't have a picture

Has a future
Shows nothing but is

Surpassing in beauty
Cannot pose a question

Simply completely
Contains an answer

Pointing nowhere
Why then these lines

Who knows
Who knows

BULL'S-EYE

What was going on that day?
Mind or was it body pulling the bow
Taut, the way she taught me to

A moment ago, who couldn't believe
Her eyes and thought she knew
I didn't believe it possible to hit

The target (how does anyone
Know what can be so), who
With a nod of encouragement

Made it clear without a word
She didn't think I ever
Would—let alone

The center, the very heart,
Standing there as if I alone
Were the target, its eye

Becoming the center of my being
In the whir of time it took
That arrow to leave the bow, to reach

What I became for an instant (oh
Yes, oh no), certain then
Of how to arrive again

At the absolute core, knowing,
As I loaded another arrow,
Lifting the bow, it would be impossible

To convey what I imagined (before
Letting the string go) to make it so.

FOR METKA

To dance
On the throat of a deer
To be slain to be spoken

Alive in a wounded wood
Each branch a line of song
Each bird a burning leaf

To step into dawn
Unsteady unbroken
Willing as a fawn about to leap

OCTOBER STORM

How can I do justice to that hive of light,
Leave-taking's blush in the maple, more
Than anything any more words may say?

No vowel endures the cold so thoroughly,
No consonant dies with such finesse
Before it falls. To close one's eyes

May be another way to store the gold
Particularity of those leaves swarming,
Fed by a wish winter will not diminish,
No matter when I wake to find what's left.

DECEMBER TANKA

Light snow, bare branches.
It's easier now to see
Deep into the woods,
Loss upon loss settling
Under a lattice of ice.

ORB

An orb of light afloat on my father's hair,
On a black wave, gentle, thick as night,
Death sound asleep in its lair,

Waiting, waiting another year.
One day, when I was older,
He told me how the glimmer

Of something he couldn't see
Enthralled my sight as he held me
In the air, above his shoulder—

Was it fear, or was it wonder?
He carried me in his arms to a mirror,
Looking until he saw what could be

The source of my newborn delight:
A waterdrop clinging to his hair
After his morning shower,

One bright orb gleaming there.
O globe of light
On a wave of my father's hair,

A wave on a wave on a wave
No longer here.

WOODEN SPOON

It is good to cook with a wooden spoon.
Heat doesn't travel from the pot
To the handle and burn one's hand,
The utensil doesn't transfer hot or cold

To or from what it is stirring.
Oh to be like that—not adding
Or subtracting anything.

But once I was: watching, outside
Always, away from others, not mixing
In their business, not involving
My body or self in theirs.

Those were the days
I wished to live an ordinary life,
With emotions extreme and mundane.

However temperate I appeared,
Inside was a storm and a sea.
However much I wished to be a part of,
To partake in, a wall prevented entry.

Oh to be a wooden spoon,
Stirring, stirring.
One day the world broke through

And I broke through
To the world. Then the trouble
Started, and something else happened
(Why *then,* I don't know, only that it did):

My desire matched another's,
Impossible match
Flaring momentarily, a force

That couldn't be reckoned with,
Ignored or properly fed. Much drama
Ensued, though nothing criminal,
Nothing that would get into the paper.

All at once I was the boiling liquid
Lapping at a frozen pond, no longer
A petrified sapling beyond burning.

Perhaps this was ordinary, too,
Only seeming extraordinary,
Out of proportion, due to a lack of
Perspective (the previously reported

Position of neutrality). It was as if
Instead of growing little by little,
Like any other infant creature,

A fully formed being
Tried to hatch from its shell,
Making the birth more violent, more
Difficult than usual. The sound

Of that hard shell cracking, sharp
Shards shattering—I hear it still,
Feel the pressure, the push and pull.

It is good to be a wooden spoon
And not be broken.
A wooden spoon stirring,
Stirring, changes everything.

NOTES

"Moroni's Tailor": Giovanni Battista Moroni (1520/24–1579) is one of the earliest painters to depict the psychological states of his sitters. *Il Sarto* or *Il Tagliapanni* (oil on canvas), in the collection of The National Gallery, London, portrays a tailor or cloth merchant; it is the first known portrait of a laborer at his trade. Most of Moroni's other subjects were members of the local aristocracy, the bourgeoisie, or the clergy. Son of Andrea Moroni, a stonemason and architect, Moroni was born in Albino and resided there most of his life. For several years he lived in the fashionable city of Bergamo, where he had a circle of patrons, but violent feuds between noble families provoked a return to his native town. Moroni's work was often misattributed; after the British rediscovered him in the nineteenth century, his reputation began to flourish.

"Woman Washing a Street in Delft" alludes to one of Vermeer's lost paintings.

"Duel of Roses" is for Veronica Piraccini, an artist from Rome, where we became friends while I lived there from June 2000 through January 2001. To usher in the third millennium, Pope John Paul II decreed the year 2000 as The Great Jubilee: a vast number of pilgrims from around the world visited Rome that year.

"Undeveloped Negatives" is dedicated to Steffen and Sana'a, who welcomed me into their home in Cairo, Egypt, in the first week of January 2001.

"Narcissus" is a reverse tanka.

"Wallpaper Poem" is dedicated to Rod Pleasants.

"Burble": Except for the four words in parenthesis, this poem is composed of definitions of *burble* and *purl* found on Vocabulary.com, an online educational service (definitions accessed on 21 June 2020).

"Ancient Story" arose from an abiding interest in microbes. Written in May 2019, this prose poem may now seem to concern SARS-CoV-2, the strain of coronavirus causing the COVID-19 pandemic.

"A Growl": Corkscrew Swamp Sanctuary, an Audubon preserve in the western Everglades, occupies more than 13,000 acres consisting mostly of wetlands; its boardwalk trail is 2.25 miles long. The Sanctuary is a natural habitat for many species of wading birds, songbirds, and raptors, as well as for otters and alligators, and includes the largest surviving virgin bald cypress forest in the world.

"Bull's-Eye" is in memory of Betty Logan (1940–1999), an athletic coach at The Kimberley School in Montclair, New Jersey, and later at Princeton University and Rutgers University. Logan was born in Birmingham, England. As an infant she was removed from her parents' custody when the *Luftwaffe* began its bombing raids across Britain; she was raised in orphanages in Scotland and never saw her parents again. One of Scotland's top young track stars, a few years after graduating university Logan moved to the United States to begin her career as a field hockey and lacrosse coach.

"For Metka" responds to one work in a suite of drawings by Metka Krašovec (1941–2018), a painter and graphic artist from Slovenia. Each image in the series invokes a different poem by Emily Dickinson: "For Metka" refers to Krašovec's drawing inspired by poem #165 ("A Wounded Deer—leaps highest—").

ACKNOWLEDGMENTS

The author wishes to thank the editors of the following journals and anthologies in which these poems, sometimes in different form, first appeared:

The Atlantic: "Chamber," "Hat Saga"
The Common: "December Tanka"
The Kenyon Review: "Ear of Corn"
Great River Review: "Burble"
Michigan Quarterly Review: "Evening Walk," "Metamorphosis," "Undeveloped Negatives"
The New Criterion: "Duel of Roses"
The New Republic: "October Storm"
The New Yorker: "September First Again," "Wallpaper Poem"
Plume: "A Growl," "Ancient Story," "A Tree in Early March," "Blueprint," "Bounty," "Giacometti's Shadow," "How It Is," "In a Valley," "Mapmakers: A Sketch," "Riddle," "Theorems of Reason," "To a New Chair"
Poetry: "An Anthology of Rain"
Poem-a-Day (Academy of American Poets): "Kettle"
Raritan: "Bull's-Eye," "Man in Red Shoes," "Orb," "Wooden Spoon"
The Yale Review: "Moroni's Tailor"

"An Anthology of Rain," translated into Czech by Sebastian Kantor, was published in *Časopis Poezie,* Issue 1 (Spring 2018).

"Narcissus" (under the title "Daffodil After a Storm") appears in *Your Echo Comes Back in Greek: A Festschrift in Honor of Rosanna Warren,* published in 2023.

"For Metka" (under the title "Doe") was published in *The Heart's Many Doors: American Poets Respond to Metka Krašovec's Images Responding to Emily Dickinson.* Edited by Richard Jackson; illustrations by Metka Krašovec. San Antonio, Texas: Wings Press, 2017.

"Contentment" was published in *The Plume Anthology of Poetry 5* (MadHat Press, 2017), "Woman Washing a Street in Delft" in *The Plume Anthology of Poetry 7* (Canisy Press, 2019), "He Returns" in *The Plume Anthology of Poetry 8* (Canisy Press, 2020), and "Light Meter" in *The Plume Anthology of Poetry 9* (Canisy Press, 2021); all editions were edited by Daniel Lawless.

"Secret Rites" originally appeared in *Fast Fierce Women: 75 Essays of Flash Nonfiction,* edited by Gina Barreca (Woodhall Press, 2022).

Immense gratitude to Daniel Lawless, Molly Peacock, Christopher Ricks, Elizabeth Spires, and Rosanna Warren for their support and criticism. I wish to acknowledge Hofstra University for granting a special leave to complete part of this collection. Special thanks to Peter Covino, Sharon Dolin, and Rachel Rothenberg of Barrow Street Press. As ever, profound thanks to JSS, my closest reader.

Photo by Sigrid Estrada

PHILLIS LEVIN was born in Paterson, New Jersey, and educated at Sarah Lawrence College and The Johns Hopkins University. She is the author of five previous poetry collections, including, most recently, *Mr. Memory & Other Poems*, a finalist for the Los Angeles Times Book Prize, and is the editor of *The Penguin Book of the Sonnet*. Winner of the Poetry Society of America's Norma Farber First Book Award, she is the recipient of a Fulbright Scholar Award to Slovenia and fellowships from the Ingram Merrill Foundation, the John Simon Guggenheim Memorial Foundation, the National Endowment for the Arts, and the Trust of Amy Lowell. She has been awarded residencies to the American Academy in Rome, Bogliasco, MacDowell, Virginia Center for the Creative Arts, and Yaddo. Her work has appeared in *AGNI, The Atlantic, The Best American Poetry, Kenyon Review, The Nation, The New Republic, The New York Times Sunday Magazine, The New Yorker, Paris Review, Plume, Poetry, Poetry London, Raritan, The Yale Review*, and elsewhere. Levin has taught at the University of Maryland and New York University and is Professor of English and Poet-in-Residence Emerita at Hofstra University. She lives with her husband in New York City and West Cornwall, Connecticut.

BARROW STREET POETRY

An Anthology of Rain
Phillis Levin 2025

Unlikely Skylight
Hollis Kurman 2025

The Mouth Is Also a Compass
Carrie Bennett 2024

Brutal Companion
Ruben Quesada 2024

Brother Nervosa
Ronald Palmer 2024

The Fire Road
Nicholas Yingling 2024

Close Red Water
Emma Aylor 2023

Fanling in October
Pui Ying Wong 2023

Landscape with Missing River
Joni Wallace 2023

Down Low and Lowdown…
Timothy Liu 2023

*the archive is all
in present tense*
Elizabeth Hoover 2022

Person, Perceived Girl
A.A. Vincent 2022

Frank Dark
Stephen Massimilla 2022

Liar
Jessica Cuello 2021

*On the Verge of Something
Bright and Good*
Derek Pollard 2021

*The Little Book of
No Consolation*
Becka Mara McKay 2021

Shoreditch
Miguel Murphy 2021

Hey Y'all Watch This
Chris Hayes 2020

Uses of My Body
Simone Savannah 2020

Vortex Street
Page Hill Starzinger 2020

*Exorcism Lessons
in the Heartland*
Cara Dees 2019

American Selfie
Curtis Bauer 2019

Hold Sway
Sally Ball 2019

Green Target
Tina Barr 2018

Luminous Debris: New &
Selected Legerdemain
Timothy Liu 2018

We Step into the Sea: New and
Selected Poems
Claudia Keelan 2018

Adorable Airport
Jacqueline Lyons 2018

Whiskey, X-ray, Yankee
Dara-Lyn Shrager 2018

For the Fire from the Straw
Heidi Lynn Nilsson 2017

Alma Almanac
Sarah Ann Winn 2017

A Dangling House
Maeve Kinkead 2017

Noon until Night
Richard Hoffman 2017

Kingdom Come Radio Show
Joni Wallace 2016

In Which I Play the Run Away
Rochelle Hurt 2016

The Dear Remote
Nearness of You
Danielle Legros Georges 2016

Detainee
Miguel Murphy 2016

Our Emotions Get Carried Away
Beyond Us
Danielle Cadena Deulen 2015

Radioland
Lesley Wheeler 2015

Tributary
Kevin McLellan 2015

Horse Medicine
Doug Anderson 2015

This Version of Earth
Soraya Shalforoosh 2014

Unions
Alfred Corn 2014

O, Heart
Claudia Keelan 2014

Last Psalm at Sea Level
Meg Day 2014

Vestigial
Page Hill Starzinger 2013

You Have to Laugh:
New + Selected Poems
Mairéad Byrne 2013

Wreck Me
Sally Ball 2013

Blight, Blight, Blight,
Ray of Hope
Frank Montesonti 2012

Self-evident
Scott Hightower 2012

Emblem
Richard Hoffman 2011

Mechanical Fireflies
Doug Ramspeck 2011

Warranty in Zulu
Matthew Gavin Frank 2010

Heterotopia
Lesley Wheeler 2010

This Noisy Egg
Nicole Walker 2010

Black Leapt In
Chris Forhan 2009

Boy with Flowers
Ely Shipley 2008

Gold Star Road
Richard Hoffman 2007

Hidden Sequel
Stan Sanvel Rubin 2006

Annus Mirabilis
Sally Ball 2005

A Hat on the Bed
Christine Scanlon 2004

Hiatus
Evelyn Reilly 2004

3.14159+
Lois Hirshkowitz 2004

Selah
Joshua Corey 2003

Pioneer Preachers in Paradise